I0448410

March 2013

INFORMATION SECURITY

IRS Has Improved Controls but Needs to Resolve Weaknesses

G A O
Accountability ★ Integrity ★ Reliability

GAO-13-350

INFORMATION SECURITY

IRS Has Improved Controls but Needs to Resolve Weaknesses

GAO

Accountability * Integrity * Reliability

Highlights

Highlights of GAO-13-350, a report to the Acting Commissioner, Internal Revenue

Why GAO Did This Study

The Internal Revenue Service (IRS) has a demanding responsibility in collecting taxes, processing tax returns, and enforcing the nation's tax laws. It relies extensively on computerized systems to support its financial and mission-related operations and on information security controls to protect the financial and sensitive taxpayer information that resides on those systems.

As part of its audit of IRS's fiscal years 2012 and 2011 financial statements, GAO assessed whether controls over key financial and tax-processing systems are effective in ensuring the confidentiality, integrity, and availability of financial and sensitive taxpayer information. To do this, GAO examined IRS information security policies, plans, and procedures; tested controls over key financial applications; and interviewed key agency officials at eight sites.

What GAO Recommends

GAO recommends that IRS take four actions to more effectively implement portions of its information security program. In a separate report with limited distribution, GAO is recommending that IRS take 30 specific actions to address newly identified control weaknesses. In commenting on a draft of this report, IRS agreed to develop a detailed corrective action plan to address each recommendation.

View GAO-13-350. For more information, contact Nancy R. Kingsbury at (202) 512-2700 or kingsburyn@gao.gov or Gregory C. Wilshusen at (202) 512-6244 or wilshuseng@gao.gov.

What GAO Found

IRS continued to make progress in addressing information security control weaknesses, improving its internal control over financial reporting. During fiscal year 2012, IRS management devoted attention and resources to addressing information security controls, and resolved a significant number of the information security control deficiencies that GAO previously reported. Notable among these efforts were the (1) formation of cross-functional working groups tasked with the identification and remediation of specific at-risk control areas, (2) improvement in controls over the encryption of data transferred between accounting systems, and (3) upgrades to critical network devices on the agency's internal network system. However, serious weaknesses remain that could affect the confidentiality, integrity, and availability of financial and sensitive taxpayer data. For example, the agency had not always (1) implemented effective controls for identifying and authenticating users, such as enforcing password complexity on certain servers; (2) appropriately restricted access to its mainframe environment; (3) effectively monitored the mainframe environment; or (4) ensured that current patches had been installed on systems to protect against known vulnerabilities.

An underlying reason for these weaknesses is that IRS has not effectively implemented portions of its information security program. The agency has established a comprehensive framework for the program, and continued to make strides with various initiatives designed to improve its controls; however, certain components of the program did not always function as intended. For example, IRS's testing procedures over a financial reporting system that GAO reviewed did not always determine whether required controls were operating effectively and consequently, GAO identified control weaknesses that had not been detected by IRS. In addition, the agency had not updated an important policy concerning security standards for IRS's main tax processing environment to include current software versions and control capabilities. Further, although IRS indicated that it had addressed 58 of the previous information system security-related recommendations GAO made, 13 (about 22 percent) of the 58 had actually not yet been fully resolved. Continued and consistent management commitment and attention to an effective information security program will be essential to the maintenance of, and continued improvements in, its information system controls. Until IRS takes additional steps to (1) more effectively implement its testing and monitoring capabilities, (2) ensure that policies and procedures are updated, and (3) address unresolved and newly identified control deficiencies, its financial and taxpayer data will remain vulnerable to inappropriate use, modification, or disclosure, possibly without being detected. These deficiencies, along with shortcomings in the information security program, were the basis of GAO's determination that IRS had a significant deficiency in its internal control over financial reporting systems for fiscal year 2012.

Contents

Abbreviations

CIO	chief information officer
ESAT	Enterprise Security Audit Trails
FISMA	Federal Information Security Management Act
IRS	Internal Revenue Service
NIST	National Institute of Standards and Technology
TIGTA	Treasury Inspector General for Tax Administration

This is a work of the U.S. government and is not subject to copyright protection in the United States. The published product may be reproduced and distributed in its entirety without further permission from GAO. However, because this work may contain copyrighted images or other material, permission from the copyright holder may be necessary if you wish to reproduce this material separately.

United States Government Accountability Office
Washington, DC 20548

March 15, 2013

Steven Miller
Acting Commissioner of Internal Revenue

Dear Mr. Miller:

The Internal Revenue Service (IRS) has a demanding responsibility in collecting taxes, processing tax returns, and enforcing the nation's tax laws. It relies extensively on computerized systems to support its financial and mission-related operations and on information security controls[1] to protect the confidentiality, integrity, and availability of the financial and sensitive taxpayer information that resides on those systems.

In each of our previous audits of IRS's financial statements, we have reported a material weakness in internal control over information security because of multiple deficiencies we found that collectively resulted in IRS being unable to rely on its financial reporting systems or compensating and mitigating controls to provide reasonable assurance that its financial statements were fairly presented.[2] These deficiencies also limited IRS's ability to provide reasonable assurance that the financial information necessary to make management decisions was reliable and the information processed by its automated systems was appropriately safeguarded.

---

[1] Information security controls include logical and physical access controls, configuration management, segregation of duties, and continuity of operations. These controls are designed to ensure that access to data is appropriately restricted, physical access to sensitive computing resources and facilities is protected, only authorized changes to computer programs are made, incompatible duties are segregated among individuals, and back-up and recovery plans are adequate and tested to ensure the continuity of essential operations.

[2] A material weakness is a deficiency, or a combination of deficiencies, in internal control such that there is a reasonable possibility that a material misstatement of the entity's financial statements will not be prevented, or detected and corrected on a timely basis. A deficiency in internal control exists when the design or operation of a control does not allow management or employees, in the normal course of performing their assigned functions, to prevent or detect and correct misstatements on a timely basis. Materiality represents the magnitude of an omission or misstatement of an item in a financial report that when considered in light of surrounding circumstances, makes it probable that the judgment of a reasonable person relying on the information would have been changed or influenced by the inclusion or correction of the item.

As part of our audit of IRS's fiscal years 2012 and 2011 financial statements,[3] we assessed the effectiveness of the agency's information security controls over its key financial and tax-processing systems, information, and interconnected networks at eight locations. These systems support the processing, storage, and transmission of financial and sensitive taxpayer information. In our report on IRS's fiscal years 2012 and 2011 financial statements, we reported that the IRS had made important progress in addressing information system-related internal control deficiencies, particularly those involving its networks and systems, which had previously reduced the overall effectiveness of IRS's information security controls and therefore the reliability of its financial data. Notable among these efforts were the (1) formation of cross-functional working groups tasked with the identification and remediation of specific at-risk control areas, (2) improvement in controls over the encryption of data transferred between accounting systems, and (3) upgrades to critical network devices on the agency's internal network system.

However, the remaining deficiencies in information security, along with new deficiencies we identified during this year's audit and discussed in this report, while not collectively considered a material weakness, are important enough to merit the attention of those charged with governance of IRS. Therefore, we reported that these issues represent a significant deficiency in IRS's internal control over financial reporting systems as of September 30, 2012.[4]

Our objective was to determine whether IRS's controls over key financial and tax processing systems are effective in ensuring the confidentiality, integrity, and availability of financial and sensitive taxpayer information. To do this, we examined the agency's information security policies, plans, and procedures; tested controls over key financial applications; interviewed key agency officials; and reviewed our prior reports to identify previously-reported weaknesses and assessed the effectiveness of corrective actions taken. Our evaluation was limited to systems relevant

---

[3]GAO, *Financial Audit: IRS's Fiscal Years 2012 and 2011 Financial Statements*, GAO-13-120 (Washington, D.C.: Nov. 9, 2012).

[4]A significant deficiency is a deficiency, or a combination of deficiencies, in internal control that is less severe than a material weakness, yet important enough to merit the attention of those charged with governance.

to financial management and reporting and was concentrated on threats emanating from sources internal to IRS's computer networks.

We conducted this audit from March 2012 to March 2013 in accordance with generally accepted government auditing standards. We believe our audit provides a reasonable basis for our opinions and other conclusions. For additional information about our objective, scope, and methodology, refer to appendix I.

Background

The use of information technology has created many benefits for agencies such as IRS in achieving their missions and providing information and services to the public, but extensive reliance on computerized information also creates challenges in securing that information from various threats. Information security is especially important for government agencies, where maintaining the public's trust is essential.

Without proper safeguards, computer systems are vulnerable to individuals and groups with malicious intentions who can intrude and use their access to obtain sensitive information, commit fraud, disrupt operations, or launch attacks against other computer systems and networks. Cyber-based threats to information systems and cyber-related critical infrastructure can come from sources internal and external to the organization. Internal threats include errors or mistakes, as well as fraudulent or malevolent acts by employees or contractors working within an organization. External threats include the ever-growing number of cyber-based attacks that can come from a variety of sources such as hackers, criminals, and foreign nations. Our previous reports, and those by federal inspectors general, describe persistent information security weaknesses that place federal agencies, including IRS, at risk of disruption, fraud, or inappropriate disclosure of sensitive information. Accordingly, we have designated information security as a governmentwide high-risk area since 1997, a designation that remains in force today.[5]

---

[5]GAO, *High-Risk Series: Information Management and Technology*, GAO/HR-97-9 (Washington, D.C.: February 1997) and *High-Risk Series: An Update*, GAO-13-283 (Washington, D.C.: February 2013).

Information security is essential to creating and maintaining effective internal controls. The Federal Managers' Financial Integrity Act of 1982[6] requires the Comptroller General to prescribe standards for internal control in federal agencies. The standards provide the overall framework for establishing and maintaining internal control and for identifying and addressing major performance and management challenges and areas at greatest risk of fraud, waste, abuse, and mismanagement.[7] The term internal control is synonymous with the term management control, which covers all aspects of an agency's operations (programmatic, financial, and compliance). The attitude and philosophy of management toward information systems can have a profound effect on internal control. Information system controls consist of those internal controls that are dependent on information systems processing and include general controls (security management, access controls, configuration management, segregation of duties, and contingency planning) at the entity, system, and business process application levels; business process application controls (input, processing, output, master file, interface, and data management system controls); and user controls (controls performed by people interacting with information systems).

Recognizing the importance of securing federal agencies' information systems, Congress enacted the Federal Information Security Management Act of 2002 (FISMA)[8] to strengthen the security of information and systems within federal agencies. FISMA requires each agency to develop, document, and implement an agencywide information security program for the information and information systems that support the operations and assets of the agency, using a risk-based approach to information security management. Such a program includes assessing risk; developing and implementing cost-effective security plans, policies, and procedures; providing security awareness and specialized training; testing and evaluating the effectiveness of controls; planning, implementing, evaluating, and documenting remedial actions to address information security deficiencies; and ensuring continuity of operations. The act also assigned to the National Institute of Standards and

---

[6]See 31 U.S.C. § 3512(c) and (d).

[7]GAO, *Standards for Internal Control in the Federal Government*, GAO/AIMD-00-21.3.1 (Washington, D.C.: November 1999).

[8]FISMA was enacted as title III, E-Government Act of 2002, Pub L. No. 107-347, Dec. 17, 2002.

GAO-13-350 IRS Information Security

Technology (NIST) the responsibility for developing standards and guidelines that include minimum information security requirements.

IRS Is the Tax Collector for the United States

IRS collects taxes, processes tax returns, and enforces federal tax laws. In fiscal years 2012 and 2011, IRS collected about $2.5 trillion and $2.4 trillion, respectively, in federal tax payments, processed hundreds of millions of tax and information returns, and paid about $373 billion and about $416 billion, respectively, in refunds to taxpayers. Further, the size and complexity of IRS add unique operational challenges. IRS employs more than 100,000 people in its Washington, D.C., headquarters and more than 650 offices in all 50 states and U.S. territories and in some U.S. embassies and consulates. IRS relies extensively on computerized systems to support its financial and mission-related operations. To manage its data and information, the agency operates three enterprise computing centers located in Detroit, Michigan; Martinsburg, West Virginia; and Memphis, Tennessee. IRS also collects and maintains a significant amount of personal and financial information on each U.S. taxpayer. Protecting the confidentiality of this sensitive information is paramount; otherwise, taxpayers could be exposed to loss of privacy and to financial loss and damages resulting from identity theft or other financial crimes.

The Commissioner of Internal Revenue has overall responsibility for ensuring the confidentiality, integrity, and availability of the information and information systems that support the agency and its operations. FISMA requires the Chief Information Officer (CIO) or comparable official at a federal agency to be responsible for developing and maintaining an information security program. IRS has delegated this responsibility to the Associate CIO for Cybersecurity, who heads the Office of Cybersecurity. The Office of Cybersecurity's mission is to protect taxpayer information and the IRS's systems, services, and data from internal and external cybersecurity-related threats by implementing security practices in planning, implementation, risk management, and operations. IRS develops and publishes its information security policies, guidelines, standards, and procedures in its *Internal Revenue Manual* and other documents in order for IRS divisions and offices to carry out their respective responsibilities in information security. In October 2012, the Treasury Inspector General for Tax Administration (TIGTA) stated that security of taxpayer data, including securing computer systems, was the top priority in its list of top 10 management challenges for IRS in fiscal year 2013.[9]

IRS Has Made Progress, but Control Weaknesses Continue to Place Financial and Taxpayer Information at Risk

IRS had implemented numerous controls over its systems, including controls for identification and authentication, authorization, cryptography, audit and monitoring, physical security, configuration management, and contingency planning. However, it had not always effectively implemented access and other controls to protect the confidentiality, integrity, and availability of its financial systems and information. These weaknesses and others in IRS's security program increase the risk that taxpayer and other sensitive information could be disclosed or modified without authorization.

Access Control Deficiencies Reduced Security over Systems

A basic management objective for any organization is to protect the resources that support its critical operations from unauthorized access. Organizations accomplish this objective by designing and implementing controls that are intended to prevent, limit, and detect unauthorized access to computing resources, programs, information, and facilities.

Access controls include those related to user identification and authentication, authorization, cryptography, audit and monitoring, and physical security. However, IRS did not fully implement effective controls in these areas. Without adequate access controls, unauthorized individuals may be able to log in, access sensitive information, and make undetected changes or deletions for malicious purposes or personal gain. In addition, authorized individuals may be able to intentionally or unintentionally view, add, modify, or delete data they should not have been given access to.

Controls for Identifying and Authenticating Users were Inconsistently Implemented

A computer system needs to be able to identify and authenticate each user or system so that activities can be linked and traced to a specific individual or system. An organization does this by assigning a unique account to each user or process, and in so doing, the system is able to distinguish one user or process from another—a process called identification. The system also needs to establish the validity of a claimed

---

[9]TIGTA, *Management and Performance Challenges Facing the Internal Revenue Service for Fiscal Year 2013* (Washington, D.C.: October 2012).

identity by requesting some kind of information, such as a password—a process known as authentication. NIST also recommends using multifactor authentication to access user accounts via a network. Multifactor authentication involves using two or more factors to achieve authentication. Factors include something you know (e.g., password or personal identification number), something you have (e.g., cryptographic identification device or token), or something you are (e.g., biometric). The combination of identification and authentication—such as user account-password combinations—provides the basis for establishing accountability and for controlling access to the system. IRS's *Internal Revenue Manual* specifies security configurations for its database systems and network support systems that cover how authentications are to be performed and how passwords are to be configured. The manual also requires the use of a strong password for authentication (defined as a minimum of eight characters, containing at least one numeric or special character, and a mixture of at least one uppercase and one lowercase letter), and that passwords be set to expire every 90 days.

IRS improved identification and authentication controls for certain databases, one of their major operating systems, and network infrastructure systems. Specifically:

- some database configurations were more securely configured such that the source of user logins was more restrictive and password controls were strengthened;
- improved password controls were implemented for servers using the UNIX operating system; and
- important data transmissions used to operate their network infrastructure were authenticated.

However, a number of identification and authentication control weaknesses continued to reduce IRS's ability to effectively control access to systems and data. For example:

- authentication controls for certain databases were not set to prevent certain vulnerabilities;
- passwords were stored without adequate controls to prevent them from being disclosed; and
- controls over complexity and age of passwords for some databases were not adequate.

Further, the agency sometimes used passwords that could be easily guessed and had not changed some passwords in nearly 2 years. In addition, the username and password for a database was stored in clear text in a file that was named so that its contents were easy to guess. Unauthorized use of this username and password would expose system information and render sensitive data vulnerable to unauthorized access. The vulnerability was compounded by the fact that the unauthorized access would be virtually undetectable since no unusual system activity would be involved—the unauthorized access would be via a valid username and password. As a result of these weaknesses, IRS had reduced ability to control who was accessing its systems and data.

Although IRS Strengthened Several Authorization Controls, Other Weaknesses Limited Control Effectiveness

Authorization is the process of granting or denying access rights and permissions to a protected resource, such as a network, a system, an application, a function, or a file. A key component of granting or denying an access right is the concept of least privilege. Least privilege is a basic principle for securing computer resources and data. It means that users are granted only those access rights and permissions that they need to perform their official duties. According to NIST, access control policies and access enforcement mechanisms are employed by organizations to control access between users (or processes acting on behalf of users) and objects in the information system. Furthermore, it notes that access enforcement mechanisms are employed at the application level, when necessary, to provide increased information security for the organization. According to the *Internal Revenue Manual*, the agency should implement access control measures that provide protection from unauthorized alteration, loss, unavailability, or disclosure of information. The manual also requires that system access be granted based on the principle of least privilege, which allows access at the minimum level necessary to support a user's job duties.

IRS had strengthened several authorization controls, including:

- eliminating certain database vulnerabilities that had previously reduced the agency's ability to enforce least privilege;
- improving isolation of mainframe processing environments to more effectively restrict access;
- strengthening an application login process to prevent users from exceeding their approved access levels; and
- restricting privileges to important files stored on a network server.

However, numerous authorization control weaknesses existed in IRS's computing environment, including:

GAO-13-350 IRS Information Security

- Access privileges allowed all users of IRS's internal network to read and write files containing sensitive system information, including passwords, that were used to support automated data transfer operations between numerous systems. Unauthorized access privileges to these files jeopardized the integrity of the data and the availability of applications.
- Administrators had more access than needed in certain instances. On one server, IRS had configured multiple databases supporting different business units to operate using the same username. As a result, any administrator with access to the username could have access to all databases, exceed his or her job duties, and affect IRS's ability to control the integrity of the data.
- For one system reviewed, database administrators were inadvertently granted privileges to administer the servers used by the database.
- Although IRS had recently tested an application, and contrary to least privilege principles, users of that application could view sensitive system information by using unintended capabilities in the user interface of the application. Subsequent to our site visit, IRS officials advised us that corrective actions had been taken in the form of programming changes to the next version of the application. However, we have not verified that these actions have been completed.

Until IRS appropriately controls users' access to its systems and effectively implements its procedures for authorization, the agency has limited assurance that its information resources are being protected from unauthorized access, alteration, and disclosure.

Inconsistent Use of Data Encryption Limited Protection of Sensitive Information

Cryptography underlies many of the mechanisms used to enforce the confidentiality and integrity of critical and sensitive information. A basic element of cryptography is encryption, which is used to transform plain text into cipher text using a special value known as a key and a mathematical process known as an algorithm. According to IRS policy, the confidentiality of transmitted data must be protected by encrypting the data to prevent unauthorized disclosure. In addition, the policy states that the use of insecure protocols should be restricted because their widespread use can allow passwords, taxpayer information, and other sensitive data to be transmitted unencrypted across its internal network.

IRS has made progress in its implementation of data encryption controls, particularly in protecting sensitive information transmitted across its internal network. However, user IDs, passwords, and data continued to be transmitted frequently without encryption. Further, many of IRS's servers were configured to weakly encrypt passwords in a manner that did not effectively prevent the passwords from being disclosed during transmission. IRS officials advised us that the weak server password encryption configuration was the result of incompatibilities between some systems that had to decrypt passwords and was expected to be resolved soon after the conclusion of our audit. Until the existing weaknesses and the newly-identified weakness are corrected, IRS's ability to reliably control access to some systems and data is undermined.

Although IRS Had Enhanced its Audit and Monitoring Capabilities, Weaknesses Reduced IRS's Ability to Audit and Monitor Many Internal Systems

To establish individual accountability, monitor compliance with security and configuration management policies, and investigate security violations, it is crucial to determine what, when, and by whom specific actions have been taken on a system. Agencies accomplish this by implementing system or security software that provides an audit trail—a log of system activity—that it can use to determine the source of a transaction or attempted transaction and to monitor user activity. The way in which organizations configure system or security software determines the nature and extent of information that can be provided by the audit trail. To be effective, agencies should configure their software to collect and maintain audit trails that are sufficient to track security-relevant events. The *Internal Revenue Manual* requires that audit logging be enabled and configured on all systems to aid in the detection of security violations, performance problems, and flaws in applications. Additionally, the manual states that security controls in information systems shall be monitored on an ongoing basis.

To enhance its auditing and monitoring capabilities, IRS established several activities designed to support detection of questionable or unauthorized access to financial applications and data and to support its response. The Enterprise Security Audit Trails (ESAT) Project Management Office is designed to assist in audit and monitoring activities by detecting questionable or unauthorized access to financial applications and data. For fiscal year 2012, this office continued to implement new procedures building on its initiatives. For example, at the time of our review, the office had enabled and configured audit logging in place for 23 systems. In addition, for a key financial system, the Office of the Chief Financial Officer documented monitoring procedures, which staff used to review the key financial system's ESAT audit logs.

However, IRS did not always effectively implement audit and monitoring controls on internal systems. Specifically, the agency did not have controls in place to detect inappropriate access between the mainframe systems used for tax processing and financial management. Data stored on disks in these systems could be accessed by a user who had been allowed access to one or more processing environments, such as development, test, or production. In addition, two of IRS's testing environments that share disk storage with the tax and financial management processing environments did not have routine monitoring oversight. The agency had also not enabled logging for a database supporting an important tax-processing application. IRS had detected this shortcoming; however, corrective actions are not scheduled to be completed for more than 2 years. Further, IRS was not consistently logging administrator activity, and certain production files on the mainframe could be changed without these changes being logged.

Without effective audit and monitoring, IRS's ability to establish individual accountability, monitor compliance with security and configuration management policies, and investigate security violations is limited.

Although IRS Had Implemented Numerous Physical Security Controls, Weaknesses Reduced Control Effectiveness

Physical security controls are important for protecting computer facilities and resources from sabotage, theft, accidental or deliberate damage, and unauthorized access. These controls involve restricting physical access to computer resources, usually by limiting access to the buildings and rooms in which they are housed and periodically reviewing the access granted in order to ensure that access continues to be appropriate. At IRS, physical access control measures, such as physical access cards that are used to permit or deny access to certain areas of a facility, are vital to safeguarding facilities, computing resources, and information from internal and external threats. The *Internal Revenue Manual* requires an inventory of nonphoto ID cards at least once every 24 hours, including a signature on the inventory form to verify that the inventory has been completed. In addition, it requires access controls that safeguard assets against possible theft and malicious actions and requires department managers of restricted areas to review, validate, sign, and date the authorized access list for restricted areas on a monthly basis and then forward the list to the physical security office for review.

IRS implemented numerous physical security controls at its enterprise computing centers to safeguard assets against possible theft and malicious actions. For example, IRS ensured guard personnel consistently conducted inventories of nonphoto ID cards, and directed the guard personnel at enterprise computing centers to sign the inventories in accordance with policy. In addition, the agency sufficiently restricted access to unattended consoles within the computing centers.

However, physical security controls were not always effectively implemented. For example, visitor physical access cards to restricted areas at one computing center provided unauthorized access to other restricted areas within the center, and regular reviews of individuals with an ongoing need to access restricted areas at one of the three computing centers were not being conducted monthly to ensure that such access was still appropriate. We previously made recommendations in fiscal year 2011 to address both of these issues.[10] Because employees and visitors may be allowed inappropriate access to restricted areas, IRS has reduced assurance that its computing resources and sensitive information are being adequately protected from unauthorized access.

IRS Had Contingency Plans in Place but Weaknesses in Other Information Security Controls Introduce Risk

In addition to access controls, other controls should be in place to ensure the confidentiality, integrity, and availability of an organization's information. These controls include policies, procedures, and techniques for securely configuring information systems and planning for continuity of operations. Weaknesses in system configurations have increased the risk of unauthorized use, disclosure, modification, or loss of information to financial and tax processing systems and taxpayer data.

Inconsistent System Configurations Resulted in Preventable Vulnerabilities

Configuration management involves, among other things, (1) verifying the correctness of the security settings in the operating systems, applications, or computing and network devices and (2) obtaining reasonable assurance that systems are configured and operating securely and as intended. Patch management, a component of configuration management, is an important element in mitigating the risks associated with software vulnerabilities. When a software vulnerability is discovered, the software vendor may develop and distribute a patch or work-around to mitigate the vulnerability. Without the patch, an attacker can exploit a vulnerability not yet mitigated, and read, modify, or delete sensitive information; disrupt operations; or launch attacks against systems at another organization. Outdated and unsupported software is more vulnerable to attack and exploitation because vendors no longer provide updates, including security updates. Change control procedures, yet another component of configuration management, are important to ensure that only authorized and fully tested systems are placed in operation. To ensure that changes to systems are necessary, work as intended, and do not result in the loss of data or program integrity, such

---

[10]GAO, *Information Security: IRS Needs to Enhance Internal Control over Financial Reporting and Taxpayer Data*, GAO-11-307SU (Washington, D.C.: March 2011).

changes should be documented, authorized, tested, and independently reviewed. Accordingly, the *Internal Revenue Manual* states that IRS will manage systems to reduce vulnerabilities by promptly installing patches. Specifically, it states that security patches should be applied within 30 days, and hardware and software on network devices should be promptly maintained and updated in response to identified vulnerabilities. The manual also states that system administrators should ensure the version of the operation system being used is one for which the vendor continues to offer standardized technical support.

IRS did not always ensure its systems were securely configured, as illustrated in the following examples:

- Servers were not consistently configured to have strong controls. Eight of 19 servers reviewed lacked a security setting to enforce standard configuration updates, resulting in weaker controls for these servers.
- The agency's automated change management process could be circumvented because individuals had privileges that allowed them to make changes to mainframe applications.

IRS has made progress in replacing outdated systems but did not always apply patches to its systems in a timely manner. During fiscal year 2012, the agency replaced older systems to ensure ongoing vendor technical support. However, as we have previously reported, it did not patch its systems within 30 days.[11] For example, a database supporting tax account processing had not been patched for several months despite the issuance of critical patches and another database used for operations support was missing key patches. IRS officials stated that these situations resulted from restrictions on making changes to systems during the tax filing season. Other servers were also not patched due to system performance problems. According to IRS, these systems were patched subsequent to our site visits, but we have not yet verified this information. The agency also has an initiative underway to resolve its lack of patch management during tax filing season.

Until IRS more completely follows its change management policies and improves the timeliness of applying patches, the agency will continue to

---

[11]GAO, *Information Security: IRS Needs to Further Enhance Internal Control over Financial Reporting and Taxpayer Data*, GAO-12-393 (Washington, D.C.: March 2012).

face an increased risk that unauthorized and/or unintended system changes may not be prevented, detected, or corrected in a timely manner.

IRS Had Developed, Documented, and Implemented Contingency Plans

Contingency planning, which includes developing contingency and business continuity plans, should be performed to ensure that when unexpected events occur, essential operations can continue without interruption or can be promptly resumed, and that sensitive data are protected. NIST guidance states that agencies should develop and implement contingency plans that describe activities associated with backing up and restoring a system after a disruption or failure. The plans should be updated and include information such as contacts, resources, and description of files in order to restore the application in the event of a disaster. In addition, the plans should be tested to determine their effectiveness and the agency's readiness to execute the plans. In addition, conducting a business impact analysis is a key step in the contingency planning process. A business impact analysis is an analysis of information technology system requirements, processes, and interdependencies used to characterize system contingency requirements and priorities in the event of a significant disruption. Moreover, it correlates the system with the critical mission/business processes and services provided and, based on that information, characterizes the consequences of a disruption. The *Internal Revenue Manual* requires the agency to develop, test, and maintain information system contingency plans for all systems, and to review and update these plans. The manual also requires a business impact analysis for each system, and includes steps for completing this process. In addition, according to the manual, IRS shall implement and enforce backup procedures for all systems and information.

IRS had processes in place to ensure recovery of their information system resources through continuity of operations, which included contingency plans and their associated test plans, as well as business impact analyses. The agency had appropriately documented and maintained current contingency plans and business impact analyses, and had tested the contingency plans for each of the six major systems we reviewed, and had the appropriate back-up procedures in place to ensure recovery of its data and information system resources.

IRS Had Developed an Information Security Program but Had Not Always Effectively Implemented Elements of the Program

A key reason for the information security weaknesses in IRS's financial and tax-processing systems was that, although the agency has developed and documented a comprehensive agencywide information security program, it had not effectively implemented certain elements of its information security program.

An entitywide information security management program should establish a framework and continuous cycle of activity for assessing risk, developing and implementing effective security procedures, and monitoring the effectiveness of these procedures. FISMA requires each agency to develop, document, and implement an information security program that, among other things, includes

- periodic assessments of the risk and magnitude of harm that could result from the unauthorized access, use, disclosure, disruption, modification, or destruction of information and information systems;
- policies and procedures that (1) are based on risk assessments, (2) cost-effectively reduce information security risks to an acceptable level, (3) ensure that information security is addressed throughout the life cycle of each system, and (4) ensure compliance with applicable requirements;
- plans for providing adequate information security for networks, facilities, and systems;
- security awareness training to inform personnel of information security risks and of their responsibilities in complying with agency policies and procedures, as well as training personnel with significant security responsibilities for information security;
- periodic testing and evaluation of the effectiveness of information security policies, procedures, and practices, performed with a frequency depending on risk, but no less than annually, and that include testing of management, operational, and technical controls for every system identified in the agency's required inventory of major information systems;
- a process for planning, implementing, evaluating, and documenting remedial action to address any deficiencies in its information security policies, procedures, or practices; and
- procedures for detecting, reporting, and responding to security incidents.

Further, the current administration has made continuous monitoring of federal information systems a top cybersecurity priority. Continuous monitoring of security controls employed within or inherited by the system is an important aspect of managing risk to information from the operation and use of information systems. Conducting a thorough point-in-time assessment of the deployed security controls is a necessary but not sufficient practice to demonstrate security due diligence. An effective information security program also includes a rigorous continuous monitoring program integrated into the system development life cycle. The objective of continuous monitoring is to determine if the set of deployed security controls continue to be effective over time in light of the inevitable changes that occur. Such monitoring is intended to assist in maintaining an ongoing awareness of information security, vulnerabilities, and threats to support agency risk management decisions. The monitoring of security controls using automated support tools facilitates near real-time risk management. As described by NIST,[12] the information security continuous monitoring process for developing a continuous monitoring strategy and implementing a continuous monitoring program consists of the following steps:

- define a continuous monitoring strategy;
- establish a continuous monitoring program that determines metrics and the frequency of monitoring and assessments;
- implement the monitoring program;
- analyze security-related information and report findings;
- respond with mitigation actions or reject, avoid, transfer, or accept risk; and
- review and update the monitoring strategy and program.

According to NIST, effective continuous monitoring begins with development of a strategy that addresses requirements and activities at each organizational tier. Each tier monitors security metrics and assesses security control effectiveness with established monitoring and assessment frequencies and status reports customized to support tier-specific decision making. The *Internal Revenue Manual* states that the agency should document its continuous monitoring strategy as defined by NIST guidance.

IRS had implemented a comprehensive information security program, as illustrated by the following examples:

---

[12]NIST, *Information Security Continuous Monitoring for Federal Information Systems and Organizations, Special Publication 800-137* (Gaithersburg, Md.: September 2011).

- IRS had developed and documented an IT security risk management policy that required all sensitive applications to be periodically assessed for the risk and magnitude of harm that could result from vulnerabilities and potential threats.
- The agency had developed policies and procedures that considered risk, appropriately addressed purpose, scope, roles, responsibilities, and compliance, and were approved by management.
- IRS had developed and documented security plans for all of the major systems we reviewed that addressed policies and procedures for providing management, operational, and technical controls.
- IRS had processes in place for providing employees with security awareness and specialized training. All employees with specific security-related roles and newly-hired employees that we reviewed met or exceeded the required minimum security awareness and specialized training hours.
- The agency had implemented numerous processes for testing and evaluating the effectiveness of controls, and told us that it had previously identified many of the issues we raised in this report. IRS also tested its general ledger system for tax transactions in its current operating environment.
- IRS had completed actions to address 61 of the 118 recommendations we reported in fiscal year 2011 that were still unresolved at the time of our last review.
- IRS had a process in place to ensure that Computer Security Incident Response Center incident tickets were opened, managed, and closed in accordance with IRS's policies and procedures governing incident detection, handling, and response.

IRS had also started numerous initiatives that covered various control areas, such as addressing weak passwords, restricting network access, improving security for shared services, and ensuring regular penetration testing and vulnerability scans.

However, not all elements of IRS's information security program had been effectively implemented, as illustrated in the following examples:

- Although IRS had developed and documented information security policies and procedures covering key topics such as risk assessments, security awareness training, testing and evaluation of security controls, configuration management, continuity of operations, and incident response, shortcomings existed with policies and procedures.

- Although IRS has a specific policy limiting global access privilege assignments in a manner that allows all users to access specific files on their mainframe systems, that policy only covered one of the two methods available for granting all users access.
- IRS's audit and monitoring policies and procedures did not comprehensively address users accessing files used by one processing environment from a different environment.
- IRS's policies and procedures for installing Oracle databases allowed for all of the databases operating on a single server to be configured such that they all run under the same system account, potentially allowing users more access than needed to perform their jobs.
- IRS's policies did not cover situations where data storage is shared between systems, which creates potential for changes made in one system to affect other systems.
- IRS's security standards for systems that support tax processing and financial management contained information that was several years out of date, which had resulted in less secure system configurations.
- The agency did not have a procedure in place to reconcile certain access privileges.

- Although IRS had processes in place for providing employees with security awareness and specialized training, the agency did not always ensure that contractors received security awareness training. The *Internal Revenue Manual* requires that all new employees and contractors receive security awareness training within the first 10 working days. For fiscal year 2012, more than half of the contractors we evaluated were not in compliance with IRS' security awareness training requirement. In addition, the agency allowed contractors to complete the required training within 6 months of their start date rather than within the first 10 working days, as required. We have previously made a recommendation to address contractor security awareness training.[13]
- IRS's procedures for testing and evaluating controls were not always effective. A key element of an information security program is conducting tests and evaluations of policies, procedures, and controls to determine whether they are effective and operating as intended. However, for one financial reporting system that we reviewed, the

---

[13]GAO, *Information Security: IRS Needs to Continue to Address Significant Weaknesses*, GAO-10-355, (Washington, D.C.: March 2010).

testing methodology did not always determine whether required authentication controls were operating effectively. Testers did not verify that controls required by policy were actually implemented on the system. Consequently, we identified control weaknesses that had not been detected by IRS. Also, IRS had not identified some of the other issues raised in this report, including weaknesses involving passwords and excessive access privileges, although they were readily detectable. Additionally, IRS's mainframe security monitoring had not detected several instances of noncompliance with its policies.

- Although IRS had a process in place for evaluating and tracking remedial actions, it did not always effectively validate that corrective actions had been taken, or whether the actions addressed the weakness. The *Internal Revenue Manual* requires that IRS track the status of resolution of all weaknesses and verify that each weakness has been corrected before closing it. During the audit period, IRS informed us that it had addressed 58 of the 118 previous information system security-related recommendations we had made that remained unresolved at the end of our prior audit. However, we determined that 13 (about 22 percent) of the 58 had actually not yet been fully resolved. We previously made a recommendation to address this issue.[14]

- IRS has not fully documented its continuous monitoring strategy. The agency created a diagram that logically depicts certain information security continuous monitoring data flows and activities, had developed various standard operating procedures, and is collecting, analyzing, and reporting on certain data. However, it does not have a strategy that defines requirements and activities at each organizational tier, mission/business processes, and information systems, nor does it define monitoring and assessment metrics and frequencies.

Until IRS effectively implements all key elements of its information security program, the agency will not have reasonable assurance that computing resources are consistently and effectively protected from inadvertent or deliberate misuse, including fraud or destruction.

Conclusions

IRS has continued to make important progress in addressing information security control weaknesses, and in improving its internal control over

---

[14]GAO, *Information Security: Further Efforts Needed to Address Significant Weaknesses at the Internal Revenue Service*, GAO-07-364 (Washington, D.C.: March 2007).

financial reporting. During fiscal year 2012, IRS management devoted attention and resources to addressing information security controls, and resolved a significant number of the information security control deficiencies that we have previously reported. Nevertheless, information security weaknesses remain in access and other information system controls over IRS's financial and tax-processing systems, affecting the confidentiality, integrity, and availability of financial and sensitive taxpayer data. The financial and taxpayer information on IRS systems will remain particularly vulnerable to internal threats until the agency (1) addresses weaknesses pertaining to identification and authentication, authorization, cryptography, audit and monitoring, physical security, and configuration management and (2) effectively implements key components of its comprehensive information security program that ensure processes intended to test, monitor, and evaluate internal controls are appropriately detecting vulnerabilities, including developing and implementing a strategy for continuous monitoring efforts and improving validation of corrective actions; and policies are up-to-date, and reflect the current operating environment. These deficiencies are the basis of our determination that IRS had a significant deficiency in internal control over financial reporting related to information security in fiscal year 2012. Continued and consistent management commitment and attention to an effective information security program will be essential to the maintenance of, and continued improvements in, the agency's information security controls.

Recommendations for Executive Action

In addition to implementing our previous recommendations, we are recommending that the Acting Commissioner of Internal Revenue take the following four actions to effectively implement key components of the IRS information security program:

- Update policies and procedures to ensure that they address (1) both methods available for granting all users access to mainframe resources, (2) audit and monitoring of access from one processing environment to another, (3) use of appropriate accounts by multiple databases on a single server, (4) data storage shared between systems, (5) out-of-date security standards, and (6) reconciliation of access privileges;
- update test and evaluation methodology to ensure that it determines whether authentication controls are operating effectively;
- update mainframe test and evaluation processes to improve periodic monitoring of compliance with IRS policies; and

- fully document a continuous monitoring strategy that includes requirements and activities definitions at each organizational tier.

We are also making 30 detailed recommendations in a separate report with limited distribution. These recommendations consist of actions to be taken to correct specific information security weaknesses related to identification and authentication, authorization, cryptography, audit and monitoring, and configuration management.

Agency Comments and Our Evaluation

In providing written comments (reprinted in app. II) on a draft of this report, the Acting Commissioner of Internal Revenue stated that the security and privacy of taxpayer and financial information is of the utmost importance to the agency and that IRS will provide a detailed corrective action plan addressing each of our recommendations. Further, the Acting Commissioner stated that the integrity of IRS's financial systems continues to be sound. However, as we noted in this report, although IRS has continued to make important progress in addressing information security control weaknesses, it had not always effectively implemented access and other controls to protect the confidentiality, integrity, and availability of its financial systems and information. The effective implementation of our recommendations in this report and in our previous reports will assist IRS in protecting taxpayer and financial information.

This report contains recommendations to you. As you know, 31 U.S.C. § 720 requires the head of a federal agency to submit a written statement of the actions taken on our recommendations to the Senate Committee on Homeland Security and Governmental Affairs and to the House Committee on Oversight and Government Reform not later than 60 days from the date of the report and to the House and Senate Committees on Appropriations with the agency's first request for appropriations made more than 60 days after the date of this report. Because agency personnel serve as the primary source of information on the status of recommendations, we request that the agency also provide us with a copy of the agency's statement of action to serve as preliminary information on the status of open recommendations.

We are also sending copies of this report to the Secretary of the Treasury, the Treasury Inspector General for Tax Administration, and interested congressional parties.

If you have any questions regarding this report, please contact Nancy R. Kingsbury at (202) 512-2700 or Gregory C. Wilshusen at (202) 512-6244. We can also be reached by e-mail at kingsburyn@gao.gov and wilshuseng@gao.gov. Key contributors to this report are listed in appendix III.

Sincerely yours,

Nancy R. Kingsbury
Managing Director, Applied Research and Methods

Gregory C. Wilshusen
Director, Information Security Issues

Appendix I: Objective, Scope, and Methodology

The objective of our review was to determine whether controls over key financial and tax-processing systems were effective in protecting the confidentiality, integrity, and availability of financial and sensitive taxpayer information at the Internal Revenue Service (IRS). To do this, we examined IRS information security policies, plans, and procedures; tested controls over key financial applications; and interviewed key agency officials in order to (1) assess the effectiveness of corrective actions taken by IRS to address weaknesses we previously reported and (2) determine whether any additional weaknesses existed. This work was performed in connection with our audit of IRS's fiscal years 2012 and 2011 financial statements for the purpose of supporting our opinion on internal control over the preparation of those statements and may not be sufficient for other purposes.

To determine whether controls over key financial and tax-processing systems were effective, we considered the results of our evaluation of IRS's actions to mitigate previously reported weaknesses, and performed new audit work at the three enterprise computing centers located in Detroit, Michigan; Martinsburg, West Virginia; and Memphis, Tennessee, as well as IRS facilities in New Carrollton, Maryland; Beckley, West Virginia; Ogden, Utah; Philadelphia, Pennsylvania; and Washington, D.C. We concentrated our evaluation on threats emanating from sources internal to IRS's computer networks. Considering systems that directly or indirectly support the processing of material transactions that are reflected in the agency's financial statements, we focused our technical work on the general support systems that directly or indirectly support key financial and taxpayer information systems such as, the Integrated Financial System; Account Management System; Graphic Data Interface; Electronic Federal Payment Posting System; Online 5081; Web Requesting Tracking System and Integrated Procurement System; Custodial Detail Database—including the Net Tax Refund Report; Automated Trust Fund Recovery Systems, Automated Interface to the National Finance Center; Redesign Revenue Accounting Control System; Customer Account Data Engine; Individual Masterfiles and Business Masterfiles; and the Integrated Data Retrieval System.

Our evaluation was based on our *Federal Information System Controls Audit Manual*,[1] which contains guidance for reviewing information system

---

[1]GAO, *Federal Information System Controls Audit Manual*, GAO-09-232G (Washington, D.C.: February 2009).

controls that affect the confidentiality, integrity, and availability of
computerized information; National Institute of Standards and Technology
guidance; and IRS policies, procedures, practices, and standards. We
evaluated controls by

- testing Domain Name Servers to determine if unnecessary services
  were running and if operating systems and software were current;
- examining IRS's implementation of encryption to secure transmissions
  on its internal network;
- reviewing physical security processes and procedures at each of the
  enterprise computing centers;
- reviewing access control/privileges of user accounts to determine if
  system access was assigned based on least privilege and
  consideration of incompatible duties;
- testing the complexity, expiration, and policy for passwords on
  databases to determine if strong password management was being
  enforced;
- testing servers and network devices to determine if adequate control
  configurations were in place;
- evaluating the mainframe operating system controls that support the
  operation of applications and databases that support revenue
  accounting;
- evaluating the controls of mainframe configurations that shared disk
  storage with multiple mainframe processing environments;
- reviewing access configurations on selected systems and database
  configurations;
- examining the status of patching for selected databases and system
  components to ensure that patches are up to date;
- reviewing IRS's process for reviewing risk assessments to determine
  if risk assessments were being reviewed at least annually;
- examining documentation to determine the extent to which IRS was
  performing internal controls reviews of key financial systems; and
- testing the design of two key applications to determine if the
  applications' access controls were effective.

Using the requirements in the Federal Information Security Management
Act of 2002, which established elements for an effective agencywide
information security program, we reviewed and evaluated IRS's
implementation of its security program by

- analyzing IRS's process for reviewing risk assessments to determine
  whether the assessments were up to date, documented, and
  approved;

- reviewing IRS's policies, procedures, practices, and standards to
  determine whether its security management program was
  documented, approved, and up to date;
- reviewing IRS's system security plans for specified systems to
  determine the extent to which the plans were reviewed, and included
  information as required by NIST;
- verifying whether employees with security-related responsibilities had
  received specialized training within the year;
- analyzing documentation to determine if the effectiveness of security
  controls is periodically assessed;
- reviewing IRS's actions to correct weaknesses to determine if they
  had effectively mitigated or resolved the vulnerability or control
  deficiency;
- reviewing IRS's Computer Security Incident Response Center incident
  tickets to determine if security violations and activities were reported
  and investigated; and
- reviewing continuity-of-operations planning documentation for six
  systems to determine if such plans were appropriately documented
  and tested.

In addition, we discussed with management officials and key security
representatives, such as those from IRS's Computer Security Incident
Response Center and Office of Cybersecurity, as well as the three
computing centers, whether information security controls were in place,
adequately designed, and operating effectively.

We performed our audit from March 2012 to March 2013 in accordance
with U.S. generally accepted government auditing standards. We believe
our audit provides a reasonable basis for our opinions and other
conclusions in this report.

Appendix II: Comments from the Internal Revenue Service

DEPARTMENT OF THE TREASURY
INTERNAL REVENUE SERVICE
WASHINGTON, D.C. 20224

COMMISSIONER

March 11, 2013

Mr. Gregory C. Wilshusen
Director, Information Security Issues
U.S. Government Accountability Office
441 G Street, N.W.
Washington, DC 20548

Dear Mr. Wilshusen:

Thank you for the opportunity to comment on the draft report titled, *Information Security: IRS Has Improved Controls but Needs to Resolve Weaknesses* (GAO-13-350).

The IRS continued to make improving information security a top priority during Fiscal Year 2012. We are pleased the Government Accountability Office (GAO) recognized our progress in strengthening controls over information security resulting in a downgrade of the information security material weakness.

We will review all of GAO's reported recommendations to ensure that our actions include sustainable fixes that implement appropriate security controls. We will provide the detailed corrective action plan addressing each of the recommendations with our response to the final report.

In closing, the security and privacy of all taxpayer information is of the utmost importance to us and the integrity of our financial systems continues to be sound. We appreciate your continued support and guidance as we work to address the recommendations and look forward to working with you to develop appropriate measures.

If you have any questions, please contact me or a member of your staff may contact Terence V. Milholland, Chief Technology Officer, at (202) 622-6800.

Sincerely,

Steven T. Miller
Acting Commissioner

Appendix III: GAO Contacts and Staff Acknowledgments

GAO Contacts

Nancy R. Kingsbury (202) 512-2700 or kingsburyn@gao.gov

Gregory C. Wilshusen (202) 512-6244 or wilshuseng@gao.gov

Staff Acknowledgments

In addition to the individuals named above, David Hayes and Jeffrey Knott (assistant directors), Bruce Cain, Mark Canter, Kristi Dorsey, Jennifer R. Franks, Nancy Glover, Mickie Gray, J. Andrew Long, Linda Kochersberger, Kevin Metcalfe, Eugene Stevens, Michael Stevens, and Daniel Swartz made key contributions to this report.

GAO's Mission	The Government Accountability Office, the audit, evaluation, and investigative arm of Congress, exists to support Congress in meeting its constitutional responsibilities and to help improve the performance and accountability of the federal government for the American people. GAO examines the use of public funds; evaluates federal programs and policies; and provides analyses, recommendations, and other assistance to help Congress make informed oversight, policy, and funding decisions. GAO's commitment to good government is reflected in its core values of accountability, integrity, and reliability.
Obtaining Copies of GAO Reports and Testimony	The fastest and easiest way to obtain copies of GAO documents at no cost is through GAO's website (http://www.gao.gov). Each weekday afternoon, GAO posts on its website newly released reports, testimony, and correspondence. To have GAO e-mail you a list of newly posted products, go to http://www.gao.gov and select "E-mail Updates."
Order by Phone	The price of each GAO publication reflects GAO's actual cost of production and distribution and depends on the number of pages in the publication and whether the publication is printed in color or black and white. Pricing and ordering information is posted on GAO's website, http://www.gao.gov/ordering.htm. Place orders by calling (202) 512-6000, toll free (866) 801-7077, or TDD (202) 512-2537. Orders may be paid for using American Express, Discover Card, MasterCard, Visa, check, or money order. Call for additional information.
Connect with GAO	Connect with GAO on Facebook, Flickr, Twitter, and YouTube. Subscribe to our RSS Feeds or E-mail Updates. Listen to our Podcasts. Visit GAO on the web at www.gao.gov.
To Report Fraud, Waste, and Abuse in Federal Programs	Contact: Website: http://www.gao.gov/fraudnet/fraudnet.htm E-mail: fraudnet@gao.gov Automated answering system: (800) 424-5454 or (202) 512-7470
Congressional Relations	Katherine Siggerud, Managing Director, siggerudk@gao.gov, (202) 512-4400, U.S. Government Accountability Office, 441 G Street NW, Room 7125, Washington, DC 20548
Public Affairs	Chuck Young, Managing Director, youngc1@gao.gov, (202) 512-4800 U.S. Government Accountability Office, 441 G Street NW, Room 7149 Washington, DC 20548

Please Print on Recycled Paper.

www.ingramcontent.com/pod-product-compliance
Lightning Source LLC
Chambersburg PA
CBHW080747290526
45790CB00008B/3357